Golda Meir

Awesome Activist

Golda Mabovitch was born in Kiev, Russia, on May 3, 1898. Her family was Jewish and experienced discrimination throughout their lives. At the time, Russia had many anti-Semitic people.

ACTIVITY - Unscramble the words in the sentence below to learn more about Golda.

Golda had an _____ sister, Sheyna,
               DEROL

and a _____ sister, T___,
        GERYOUN

Anti-Semitism means a hatred of Jewish people.

D1519351

Golda's father was a carpenter. Because he was Jewish, people often did not pay him for his work. It was hard for him to support his family. He decided to move to the United States in 1903. After making some money, he sent for his family in 1906.

The *U.S.* was called the "Golden Land" because of the opportunities open for people, no matter what their religion.

Where did Golda and her family settle in the *U.S.*? Solve the code to find out!

A	B	C	D	E	F	G	H	I	J	K	L	M
✸	❀	✣	♣	➳	❤	❢	✲	✂	✆	☛	✈	✉

N	O	P	Q	R	S	T	U	V	W	X	Y	Z
✿	☆	✦	✡	✎	❦	☎	✒	✚	✖	✍	✠	✓

___ ___ ___ ___ ___ ___ ___ ___ ___

✉ ✂ ✈ ✖ ✸ ✒ ☛ ➳ ➳

___ ___ ___ ___ ___ ___ ___ ___ ___

✖ ✂ ❦ ✣ ☆ ✿ ❦ ✂ ✿

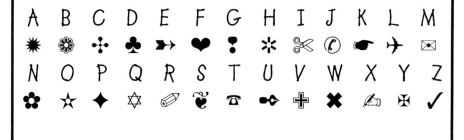

After a long and dangerous trip, Golda and her mother and sisters arrived in the U.S. Golda's father looked very different and very American. Golda enjoyed all there was to see and do in Milwaukee.

Golda's first car ride was from the railroad station to her father's apartment.

Use a mirror to read this backwards sentence.

GOLDA LOVED AMERICAN SODA POP!

_____ _____

_____

_____ _____!

Golda's mother opened a dairy store. Golda worked there every day before school.

MILK
MILK

Golda's older sister, Sheyna, eventually moved to Denver, Colorado. Golda's parents wanted Golda to quit school and marry an older man. She refused and ran away to join her sister in Colorado.

Sheyna and her husband sent Golda most of the money she needed to run away.

How old was Golda when she ran away from home? Solve the problem below to find out.

$$18-9+2+4-5+6=\underline{\hspace{2cm}} \text{ years old}$$

Golda was a good student and enjoyed school.

While in Denver, Golda attended high school. She met Morris Myerson, who would later become her husband. While still in her teens, she became a Zionist. Zionists were dedicated to building a homeland for Jews.

Put the following list of events in order.

_____ Golda runs away to Denver.
_____ Golda's family emigrates to the U.S.
_____ Golda returns to Milwaukee.
_____ Golda meets Morris Myerson.

After 2 years in Denver, Golda's father wrote her a heartfelt letter asking her to come back to Milwaukee. She did.

Golda and Morris were married in 1917. Morris worked as a sign painter. Golda traveled across the country, speaking for a group that was working to make a Jewish homeland in Palestine.

Find the words in the word search below.

PALESTINE   GOLDA   JEWISH

Palestine is in southwestern Asia. It is now called Israel.

on the MOVE
THIS END UP
FRAGILE

In 1921, Golda and Morris moved to Palestine.

T	S	I	N	O
K	I	B	B	U
G	J	D	K	H
M	E	N	I	T
H	W	B	F	Q
A	I	L	P	G
D	S	T	N	S
K	H	E	O	N

In Palestine, Golda and Morris lived in a kibbutz called Merhavyah for two years. Golda and Morris worked hard in this small community.

ISRAEL   KIBBUTZ   ZIONIST

I	Z	B	I	M
T	Z	G	S	F
J	N	O	R	C
S	E	L	A	P
U	M	D	E	G
P	W	A	L	R
C	J	V	Z	O
A	L	T	X	B

After two years, Golda and Morris moved to Jerusalem. While there, the couple had two children.

In 1947, the United Nations decided to split Palestine into an Arab and a Jewish state. Golda knew this would lead to fights between the two nations. However, she accepted many government positions for her new nation of Israel.

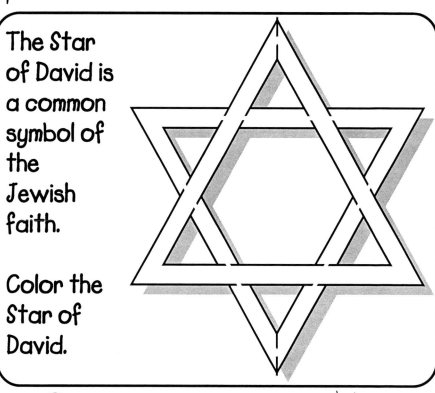

The Star of David is a common symbol of the Jewish faith.

Color the Star of David.

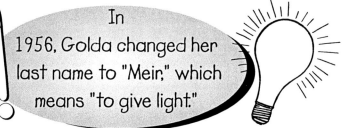

In 1956, Golda changed her last name to "Meir," which means "to give light."

In 1956, Golda became the foreign minister for Israel. She held this position until 1966, when she retired. She remained active in politics and was asked to step in as prime minister, or premier, in 1969.

Golda was Israel's first woman prime minister. She held the position for 5 years.

How old was Golda when she became prime minister of Israel? Solve the problem below to find out.

1969 (year appointed)

−1898 (year of birth)

(age at appointment)

Golda passed away on December 8, 1978, in Jerusalem. She had lived during great times of trouble for Jewish people, as well as times of celebration. Her dream of a Jewish homeland came true.

Golda died with a dream that one day the Arabs and Israelis would live in peace.

Cross off every other letter, beginning with J, to find the Jewish word for peace.

JSLHVAPLRONM

_____

My Life by Golda Meir

Golda wrote a book, *My Life*, that tells her life story.

Glossary

anti-Semitism: hatred of Jews

kibbutz: a settlement of people who share what they earn and own

minister: a high position of government

premier: a chief officer

shalom: Hebrew word for peace

Zionist: a person dedicated to making a Jewish homeland in Palestine

❁ Pop Quiz! ❁

1. In what country was Golda born?
   - ○ Russia
   - ○ United States
   - ○ Israel

2. Golda emigrated to which Wisconsin city?
   - ○ Madison
   - ○ Green Bay
   - ○ Milwaukee

3. As a teenager, Golda joined which group?
   - ○ Zionists
   - ○ Girl Scouts
   - ○ Writers' Guild

4. Golda and her husband moved to Palestine to live in a _____.
   - ○ hut
   - ○ camp
   - ○ kibbutz

5. Golda became Israel's first woman _____.
   - ○ president
   - ○ prime minister
   - ○ general